D0641049

Ariel Books

**Andrews McMeel
Publishing**

Kansas City

It's a Girl!

A Book of Quotations

EDITED BY **Mary Rodarte**

PHOTOGRAPHS BY **Julie Gang**

Photographs copyright © 1999 by Julie Gang

www.andrewsmcmeel.com

ISBN: 0-7407-0071-5
Library of Congress Catalog Card Number: 99-60622

Contents

Introduction

Congratulations on your new baby girl! Marvel at the miracle of her tiny toes and fingers. Breathe in the new baby smell of your daughter, whom you've waited for with such anticipation. You have a new

*I
T'
S

A

G
I
R
L

!*

member of your family, and a new person to get to know, to guide and protect, to teach, to laugh with, to become friends with, and most important, to love.

With this new little piece of heaven in your life, you have much to look forward to! Who is this creation you've brought into the world? What is she thinking? What would she say to you now, if only she could? You

have a lifetime to find out the answers.

As you hold your little girl in your arms, remember that it may not always be easy, but it will always be worth it. You have a daughter now, to take pleasure and pride in, to admire, and to be charmed by, as she gurgles and coos and makes eyes at her new parents. As you read this book,

celebrate and marvel at the joy of having a precious baby daughter.

Welcome,

Baby Girl!

I
T'
S

A

G
I
R
L
!

You were such a wanted baby. I would rub my belly in awe of your growing. Sit motionless waiting for your kicks and stretches. Think of you, wonder about you, wait for you—totally caught in the miracle of your coming to life. First Child, child of hope, child of commitment.

—Julie Owen Edwards

Once a child is born, it is no longer in our power not to love it nor care about it.

—Epictetus

Babies are always more trouble than you thought— and more wonderful.

—Charles Osgood

Every babe born into the world is a finer one than the last.

— Charles Dickens

I T' S   A   G I R L !

What are little girls
　　made of?
Sugar and spice, and every-
　　thing nice;
That's what little girls are
　　made of.

—Anonymous

Nobody said giving birth is
easy, but there's no other
way to get the job done.

—Ivana Trump

It sometimes happens, even in the best of families, that a baby is born. This is not necessarily cause for alarm. The important thing is to keep your wits about you and borrow some money.

—Elinor Goulding Smith

I T ' S   A   G I R L !

Then someone placed her in my arms. She looked up at me. The crying stopped. Her eyes melted through me, forging a connection in me with their soft heat.

—Shirley MacLaine

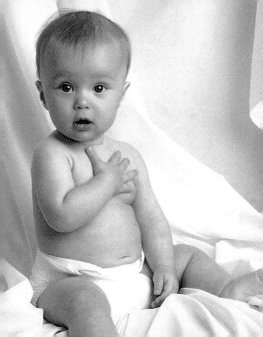

I
T'
S

A

G
I
R
L

!

In the sheltered simplicity of the first days after a baby is born, one sees again the magical closed circle, the miraculous sense of two people existing only for each other.

—Anne Morrow Lindbergh

The first, the most funda-
mental right of childhood
is the right to be loved.
The child comes into the
world alone, defenseless,
without resource. Only
love can stand between his
infant helplessness and the
savagery of a harsh world.
—Paul Hanly Furfey

Babies are such a nice way to start people.

—Don Herold

I T' S   A   G I R L !

Having a baby is like falling in love again, both with your husband and your child.

—Jane Seymour

Every child born into the world is a new thought of God, an ever fresh and radiant possibility.

—Kate Douglas Wiggin

A baby is God's opinion that the world should go on.

—Carl Sandburg

Of all the joys that lighten suffering earth, what joy is welcomed like a newborn child?

—Caroline Norton

I
T'
S

A

G
I
R
L
!

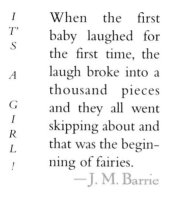

When the first baby laughed for the first time, the laugh broke into a thousand pieces and they all went skipping about and that was the beginning of fairies.

—J. M. Barrie

I T'S   A   G I R L !

I looked at this tiny, perfect creature and it was as though a light switch had been turned on. A great rush of love, mother love, flooded out of me.

—Madeleine L'Engle

Suddenly she was here.
And I was no longer preg-
nant; I was a mother. I
never believed in miracles
before.

—Ellen Greene

I T'S   A   G I R L !

No event ever in my life has been so profound, so joyful, so moving. I fell in love as I never have before or since.

—Ali MacGraw

Sleep,

Baby, Sleep

I
T'
S

A

G
I
R
L
!

The only thing worth steal-
ing is a kiss from a sleeping
child.

—Joe Houldsworth

Having children is like having a bowling alley installed
in your brain.

—Martin Mull

In the evening, after she has gone to sleep, I kneel beside the crib and touch her face, where it is pressed against the slats, with mine.
—Joan Didion

There was a little girl,
Who had a little curl
Right in the middle of
  her forehead;
And when she was good
She was very, very good,
But when she was bad
  she was horrid.

—Henry Wadsworth
      Longfellow

I
T'
S

A

G
I
R
L
!

In point of fact, we are all born rude. No infant has ever appeared yet with the grace to understand how inconsiderate it is to disturb others in the middle of the night.

—Judith Martin
("Miss Manners")

Adam and Eve had many advantages, but the principal one was that they escaped teething.
—Mark Twain

Having a baby is like living with a vampire. They sleep by day and suck the life out of you at night.
—Bobby Slayton

*I
T'
S

A

G
I
R
L
!*

No animal is so inexhaust-
ible as an excited infant.

—Amy Leslie

People who say they sleep
like a baby usually don't
have one.

—Leo J. Burke

I T'S A GIRL!

Every morning I woke up tired and angry until I realized that sleep, as I knew it, no longer existed. Now, I only wake up tired.

—Nancy Ison

The human baby, the human being, is a mosaic of animal and angel.

—Jacob Bronowski

Seeing you sleeping on your back among your stuffed ducks, bears, and basset hounds would re-mind me that no matter how good the next day might be, certain moments were gone forever.

—Joan Baez

*I
T'
S

A

G
I
R
L
!*

Insomnia: a contagious dis-
ease often transmitted from
babies to parents.

—Shannon Fife

Sleep, baby, sleep,
Thy father guards the sheep;
Thy mother shakes the
    dreamland tree,
And from it fall sweet
    dreams for thee.
Sleep, baby, sleep.

—Nursery rhyme

Mothers and

Daughters

Our daughters are the
most precious of our trea-
sures, the dearest posses-
sions of our homes and
the objects of our most
watchful love.
—Margaret E. Sangster

Being a daughter is only
half the equation; bearing
one is the other.
                —Erica Jong

I T'S   A   G I R L !

There is nothing more absorbing than a baby, nothing more intoxicating.

—Mary Gordon

Probably there is nothing in human nature more resonant with charges than the flow of energy between two biologically alike bodies, one of which has lain in amniotic bliss inside the other, one of which has labored to give birth to the other. The materials are here for the deepest mutuality and the most painful estrangement.

—Adrienne Rich

Who is getting more pleasure from this rocking, the baby or me?
—Nancy Thayer

Think always that, having the child at your breast, and having it in your arms, you have God's blessing there.
—Elizabeth Clinton

I
T'
S

A

G
I
R
L

!

It is a feeling of intimacy and exclusiveness . . . a warm, lazy intimate gaiety. I feel . . . a need to laugh out in triumph, because of this marvelous, precarious, immortal human being.

—Doris Lessing

From the instant I saw her, a tiny red creature bathed in the weird underwater light of the hospital operating room, I loved her with an intensity that life had not prepared me for.

—Susan Cheever

O young thing,
your mother's lovely
armful! How sweet the
fragrance of your body!

—Euripides

*I
T'
S*

A

*G
I
R
L
!*

Some of my best ideas come to me while I'm nursing my baby.

— Joyce Willaford

Now the thing about having a baby—and I can't be the first person to have noticed this—is that thereafter you *have* it.

— Jean Kerr

My daughter's birth was the incomparable gift of seeing the world at quite a different angle than before and judging it by standards that would apply far beyond my natural life.

—Alice Walker

There is an amazed

5⁹

curiosity in every young mother. It is strangely miraculous to see and to hold a living being formed within oneself and issued forth from oneself.

—Simone de Beauvoir

I T' S A G I R L !

So I took my daughter in my arms and said, "I love you." I told her that she was precious to me, and I stroked her hair. She sucked her thumb and lay there like a contented cat.

—Nikki Gerrard

A babe at the breast is as much pleasure as the bearing is pain.

—Marion Zimmer Bradley

My darling little girl-child, after such a long and troublesome waiting I now have you in my arms. I am alone no more. I have my baby.

—Martha Martin

I'S A GIRL!

I, who was never quite sure about being a girl, needed another life, and another image to remind me. . . . I made you to find me.

—Anne Sexton

Daddy's

Little Girl

Little girls are the nicest things that happen to people. They are born with a little bit of angel-shine about them and though it wears thin some-times there is always enough left to lasso your heart— even when they are sitting in the mud, or crying temperamental tears, or parading up the street in mother's best clothes.

—Alan Beck

I
T'
S

A

G
I
R
L
!

It is hard to raise sons; and
much harder to raise daughters.

—Shalom Aleichem

A daughter is a treasure—
and a cause of sleeplessness.

—Ben Sirach

A good daughter is like a good piece of writing: candid, lyrical, graceful, moving, alive. I have seen a young girl walk across a room, intent on her intense errand, and it was like seeing a voice become visible, as if not her tongue but her motion said, "I will do this for my life."

—Paul Engle

In love to our wives there is desire, to our sons there is ambition; but to our daughters there is something which there are no words to express.

—Joseph Addison

I T'S A G I R L !

I've been trying to think of the last thing that awed me. . . . The only thing I can come up with is the birth of my daughter almost five years ago.

—Leonard Pitts Jr.

The whisper of a baby girl can be heard farther than the roar of a lion.

—Arab proverb

I can do one of two things. I can be president of the United States, or I can control Alice. I cannot possibly do both.
—Theodore Roosevelt

The lucky man has a daughter as his first child.
—Spanish proverb

I T' S   A   G I R L !

When it comes to little girls, God the father has nothing on father, the god. It's an awesome responsibility.

—Frank Pittman

It isn't that I'm a weak father, it's just that she's a strong daughter.

—Henry Fonda

Bringing Up

Baby

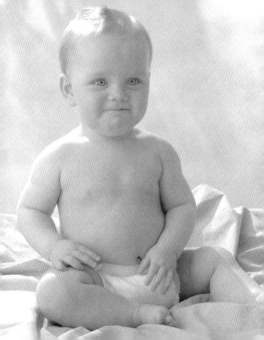

Children are the living
messages we send to a
time we will not see.

—John W. Whitehead

I'S A GIRL!

There are no seven wonders of the world in the eyes of a child. There are seven million.

—Walt Streightiff

Children, like animals, use all their senses to discover the world.

—Eudora Welty

Don't forget that compared to a grown-up person every baby is a genius. Think of the capacity to learn! The freshness, the temperament, the will of a baby a few months old!

—May Sarton

A baby is an inestimable blessing and a bother.

—Mark Twain

This book was composed in Bembo with display in Pabst.

Book design and composition by
JUDITH STAGNITTO ABBATE
of Abbate Design
Doylestown, Pennsylvania

A child is a curly, dimpled lunatic.

—Ralph Waldo Emerson

The world tips away when we look into our children's faces.

—Louise Erdrich